Welcome to Mia's adventures

By following Mia in her little adventures with her family and friends, children of all ages will discover a new beautiful language, Spanish! Little by little, step by step the grammar unfolds in front of their eyes in a simple but effective way.

These series of books have been designed with primary / elementary national curriculums in mind that make learning a foreign language compulsory at a young age.

Let Mia make learning Spanish fun!

How to use this book

- Introduce Mia and talk about the places you can see in her world.
- Look through the pictures, can you guess what is the book about?
- Encourage them to repeat the words with you and praise them frequently as they do so! This will help them to practice speaking Spanish and help them to remember new words.
- Recap regularly and return to previous words that the children have enjoyed.
- Try to use the new words learnt during your daily activities (pointing at yourself and repeat "Yo soy ... I am ...")
- HAVE FUN!

Other titles within this series available

Text and illustrations copyright © Nerea Kennedy 2022

All rights reserved. No part of this publication may be reproduced, stored in a retrieval system, distributed, or transmitted in any form or by any means, including photocopying, recording, or other electronic or mechanical methods, without the prior written permission of the publisher, except in the case of brief quotations, embodied in critical reviews and certain other noncommercial uses permitted by copyright law. Moral rights asserted.

ISBN 978-1-7398933-4-7

A catalogue record for this book is available from the British Library

Para Nahia, Ariana y Aroa ...
os quiero, os adoro, os amo mucho

Mamá

Mia

Mia's family ~ La familia de Mia

Mummy
Mamá

Daddy
Papá

Brother
Hermano

Sister
Hermana

Mia

Mia's friends ~ Los amigos de Mia

Alice   **Molly**   **Noah**   **Tom**

Oliver   **Mrs Lopez / La señora Lopez**

I am - (yo soy) ... Mia (1)
Grammar

> In Spanish there are two forms of the verb "to be", "ser" and "estar", and sometimes it can get confusing to know when to use one or the other...
>
> **Let Mia teach you** in this book the use of **"to be" / "ser"**
>
> when talking about our **own identity**

Some of the uses of "to be" in Spanish

Nationality (5)
I am English ~ Yo soy inglesa

Identity (1)
I am Mia ~ Yo soy Mia

Profession (4)
I am a teacher ~ Yo soy profesora

Physical appearance (2)
I am tall ~ Yo soy alta

Character / Personality (3)
I am intelligent ~ Yo soy inteligente

El dormitorio – The bedroom

Cama – Bed | **Mesa** – Table | **Mochila** – Rucksack | **Ventana** – Window

La cocina – The kitchen

Hola – Hello | **Mamá** – Mummy | **Buenos días** – Good morning

LA CALLE

La calle – The street

Adiós – Goodbye | **Mamá** – Mummy

La escuela – The school

Hola – Hello | **Yo soy / soy** – I am | **Buenos días** – Good morning

Hola – Hello | **Yo soy** – I am

El pasillo – The hallway
Buenos días – Good morning | **Yo soy** – I am | **Y** – And

Yo me llamo / me llamo – I am called | **Yo soy** – I am | **Y** – And

La clase – The classroom

Buenos días – Good morning | **Soy** – I am | **La señora Lopez** – Mrs Lopez
Y tú – And you | **¿Cómo te llamas?** – What's your name?

No – No | **Yo no soy** – I am not | **Yo soy** – I am

El patio – The playground

Niños – Children | **Bien hecho** – Well done

La calle – The street

Buenas tardes – Good Afternoon | **¿Cómo estás?** – How are you? | **Mamá** – Mummy
Muy bien – Very well

La cocina – The kitchen

Buenas tardes – Good afternoon | **¿Cómo estás?** – How are you? | **Papá** – Daddy

Muy bien – Very well

La cocina – The kitchen

Papá – Daddy | **Mamá** – Mummy | **Hermano** – Brother | **Hermana** – Sister

El dormitorio – The bedroom

Buenas noches – Good evening | **Fin** – The end

Vocabulary ~ Vocabulario

Places ~ Lugares

The world ~ El mundo
The mountains ~ Las montañas
The forest ~ El bosque
The lake ~ El lago
The sea ~ El mar
The river ~ El río
The waterfall ~ La cascada
The beach ~ La playa
The park ~ El parque
The cinema ~ El cine
The library ~ La biblioteca
The bakery ~ La panadería
The shops ~ Las tiendas
The school ~ La escuela
The classroom ~ La clase
The playground ~ El patio
The house ~ La casa
The bedroom ~ El dormitorio
The kitchen ~ La cocina

People ~ Gente

Mummy ~ Mamá
Daddy ~ Papá
Brother ~ Hermano
Sister ~ Hermana
Mrs ~ Señora
The teacher ~ La profesora
The family ~ La familia
The friends ~ Los amigos
Children ~ Niños

Extras

Cama ~ Bed
Mesa ~ Table
Mochila ~ Rucksack
Ventana ~ Window

Vocabulary – Vocabulario

Greetings ~ Saludos y despedidas

Hello ~ Hola
Good morning ~ Buenos días
Good afternoon ~ Buenas tardes
Good evening ~ Buenas noches
Goodbye ~ Adiós

Verbs ~ Verbos

I am…~ Yo soy
I am…~ Soy
I am not …~ Yo no soy
I am called…~ Yo me llamo
I am called…~ Me llamo

Questions? ~ ¿Preguntas?

¿? ~ Question marks
¡! ~ Exclamation marks
How are you? ~ ¿Cómo estás?
What's your name? ~ ¿Cómo te llamas?

Extras

No ~ No
You ~ Tú
And ~ Y
Very well ~ Muy bien
Well done ~ Bien hecho
Thank you ~ Gracias
The end ~ Fin

Let's practice – Ready, steady, go...

- **Encourage them to repeat** the words with you and **praise them** frequently as they do so!
- **Recap regularly** and return to previous words that the children have enjoyed.
- **Try to use the new words learnt** during **your daily activities** (pointing at yourself and repeat "Yo soy ... I am ...")
- **HAVE FUN!**

Do you remember ...

- how to say "Daddy" in Spanish? ☐
- ... and "Mummy"? ☐
- how to say "Hello" in Spanish? ☐
- ... and "Goodbye"? ☐
- how to say "Good morning" and "Good afternoon" and "Good evening" in Spanish? ☐ ☐ ☐
- how to say "I am"? ☐
- how to say "How are you?" ☐
- what are the names of Mia's girl-friends? ☐ ☐ ☐
- what are the names of Mia's boy-friends? ☐ ☐ ☐

Total points ...   / 15

Let's practice – Ready, steady, go...

Let's have a little conversation with Mia,

What would you say to her?

MIA • Hola, Buenos días

You _____

MIA • ¿Cómo te llamas?

You _____

You _____

Mia's answer ~ Me llamo Mia

MIA • ¿Cómo estás?

You_____

You_____

Mia's answer ~ Muy bien, gracias

MIA • Adiós

You _____

Let's practice – Ready, steady, go...

M	a	m	á	q	e	S
a	s	d	p	w	s	o
H	o	l	a	e	a	y
b	Y	u	P	r	l	o
A	d	i	ó	s	C	t

Can you find these words?

- Soy (I am)
- Adiós (Goodbye)
- Y (And)
- Mamá (Mummy)
- Yo (I)
- Hola (Hello)
- Clase (Classroom)
- Papá (Daddy)

Let's practice – Ready, steady, go...

Can you match the words?

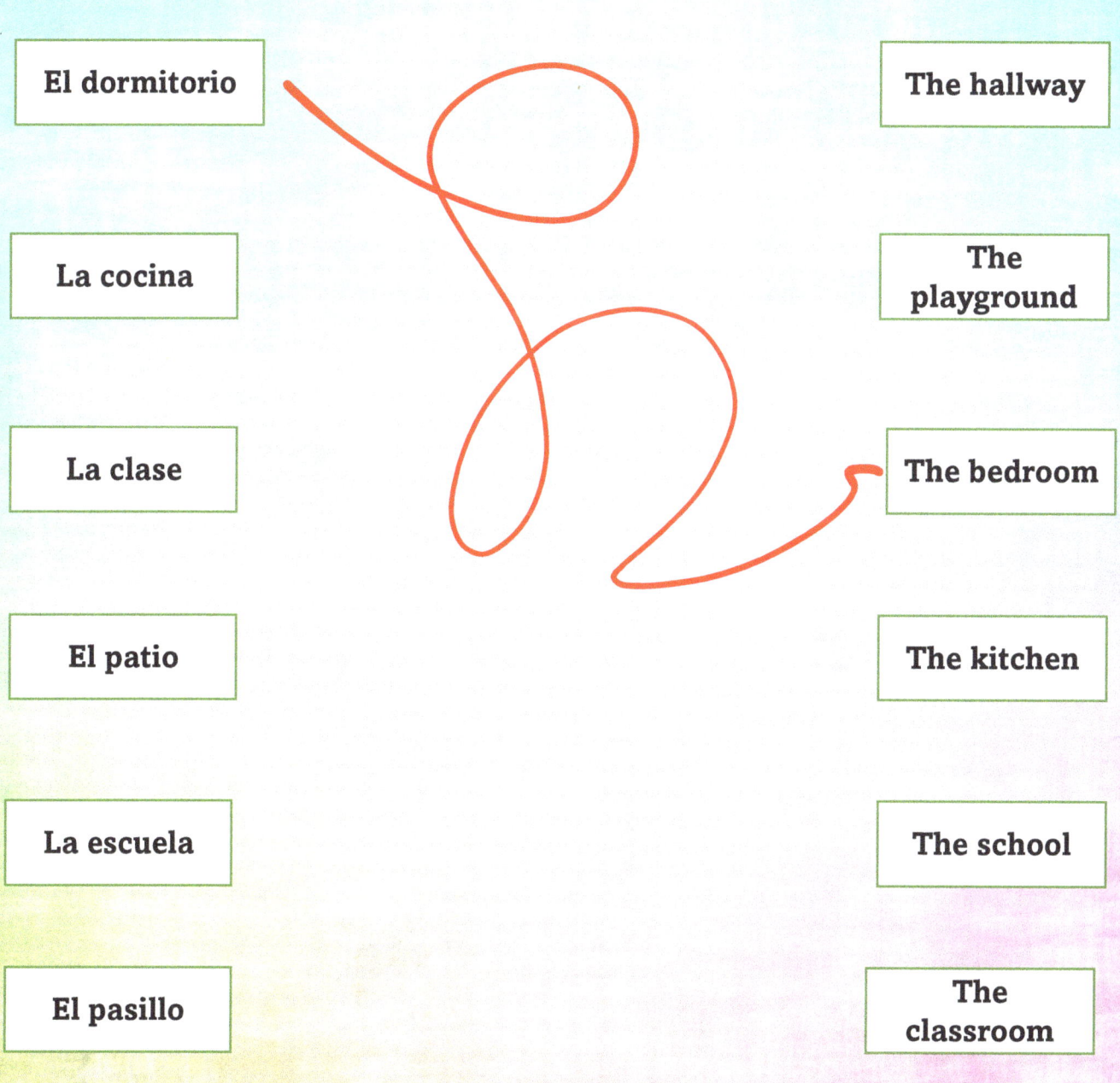

El dormitorio	The hallway
La cocina	The playground
La clase	The bedroom
El patio	The kitchen
La escuela	The school
El pasillo	The classroom

Answers

Do you remember …

- how to say "Daddy" in Spanish? **Papá**
- … and "Mummy"? **Mamá**
- how to say "Hello" in Spanish? **Hola**
- … and "Goodbye"? **Adiós**
- how to say "I am"? **Yo soy / Soy**
- how to say "How are you? **¿Cómo estás?**
- what are the names of Mia's girl-friends? **Alice and Molly**
- what are the names of Mia's boy-friends? **Noah, Oliver and Tom**
- how to say "Good morning" and "Good afternoon"
and "Good evening" in Spanish? **Buenos días ~ Buenas tardes ~ Buenas noches**

Let's have a little conversation with Mia, What would you say to her?

MIA • Hola, buenos días   You ~ Hola, buenos días

MIA • ¿Cómo te llamas?   You ~ Me llamo ……………
                                 You ~ Y tú, ¿Cómo te llamas?

Mia's answer ~ Me llamo Mia

MIA • ¿Cómo estás?   You ~ Muy bien
                                 You ~ Y tú, ¿Cómo estás?

Mia's answer ~ Muy bien, gracias

MIA • Adiós   You ~ Adiós

Answers

M	a	m	á	q	e	S
a	s	d	p	w	s	o
H	o	l	a	e	a	y
b	Y	u	P	r	l	o
A	d	i	ó	s	C	t

Can you match the words?

Mia's adventures

LEVEL 1

Learn Spanish with Mia

Series 1 – Verb to be - Verbo Ser

- I am ~ Yo soy ... - Mia – Identity (1)

I am Mia – Yo soy Mia

- I am ~ Yo soy ... - Physical appearance (2)

I am tall – Yo soy alta

- I am ~ Yo soy ... - Character / Personality (3)

I am Intelligent – Yo soy inteligente

- I am ~ Yo soy ... - Professions (4)

I am a teacher – Yo soy profesora

- I am ~ Yo soy ... - Nationality (5)

I am English – Yo soy Inglesa

- I am ~ Yo soy ... - Revision (6)

Mia's adventures

LEVEL 1

Learn Spanish with Mia

Series 1 •   To be ~ Ser

Series 2 •. To be ~ Estar

Series 3 •   To have ~ Tener

Series 4 •. To play ~ Jugar

Series 5 •   To like ~ Gustar

Series 6 •   To wear ~ Llevar (puesto)

PLUS: Animals, colours, family members, numbers and lots more!

Coming soon other titles within this series.
For extra resources, videos and lots more join our community:
www.nereakennedybooks.com
Activity books ~ Colouring books ~ Workbooks ~ Crosswords ~
Dot to dot ~ Grammar books

Other titles available Learn with Mia ...

Reading books

Grammar books

Learn French

Learn German

Colouring books

Crosswords

Learn Italian

Learn Japanese

Activity books

Workbooks

Dot to Dot

Other titles within this series available.
For extra resources, videos and lots more join our community:
www.nereakennedybooks.com

www.ingramcontent.com/pod-product-compliance
Lightning Source LLC
Chambersburg PA
CBHW051322110526
44590CB00031B/4436